Dear reader,

To read the text on this page, you need light, your eyes, and your brain. These things must work together seamlessly in order for you to see.

Sometimes this beautiful sensory system suffers from glitches. Maybe objects far away from you look blurry, or maybe words right in front of you are hard to read. Maybe there are certain colors you can't tell apart, or maybe you only see shapes and shadows. My own grandmother suffered from glaucoma and lost her ability to see at an early age. She often walked with her head turned high as if she wanted to capture as much light as possible. She liked doing things herself and was a wonderful storyteller.

In this book, I present these vision glitches and the solutions that scientists have developed to address them. Whether you are a child or an adult, I hope that this book will teach you how your own eyes work and how your friends or family might experience the world around them.

I am honored to have written this book and hope that it will help you better understand and protect your eyes, no matter what they are able to see.

Noureddine Melikechi

How Do You See the World?
Hardcover first edition • May 2024 • ISBN: 978-1-958629-43-7
eBook first edition • May 2024 • ISBN: 978-1-958629-44-4

Written by Noureddine Melikechi, Text © 2024
Illustrated by Michelle Simpson, Illustrations © 2024

Project Manager, Cover and Book Design: Hannah Thelen, Washington, D.C.
Senior Editor, Design Assistant: Caitlin Burnham, Washington, D.C.
Editor: Marlee Brooks, Washington, D.C.
Editorial Assistants: Brooke McGurl, Jordan Roller

Special thanks to our sensitivity readers Aleesha Grady, Anna Riehle, and Bonnie Hillsberg.

Spanish edition coming soon.

Teacher's Guide available at the Educational Resources page of ScienceNaturally.com.

Published by:
Science, Naturally! – An imprint of Platypus Media, LLC
    750 First Street NE, Suite 700
    Washington, DC 20002
    202-465-4798
    Info@ScienceNaturally.com • ScienceNaturally.com

Distributed to the book trade by:
    National Book Network (North America)
        301-459-3366 • Toll-free: 800-462-6420
        CustomerCare@NBNbooks.com • NBNbooks.com
    NBN International (worldwide)
        NBNi.Cservs@IngramContent.com • Distribution.NBNi.co.uk

Library of Congress Control Number: 2023949865

10 9 8 7 6 5 4 3 2 1

This book uses two fonts developed specifically for legibility or low vision: **Luciole** and **Andika**. These fonts can be found online for free!

Schools, libraries, government and non-profit organizations can receive a bulk discount for quantity orders.
Contact us at the address above or email us at Info@ScienceNaturally.com.

Printed in China.

How Do You See the World?

By Noureddine Melikechi, D.Phil.
Illustrated by Michelle Simpson

Science, Naturally!
An imprint of Platypus Media, LLC

Washington, D.C.

If you're looking at this book, you're using your eyes to see.

Seeing helps us understand the world around us. Each of us sees the world differently because of small differences in our eyes. Some people are born with these differences. Others have accidents or conditions that affect their eyes later on.

Learning how our eyes work helps us understand why we each see the world in a unique way.

To see, we need light to enter our eyes. We can't see when our eyes are closed or when it's dark out, because there is very little light. We get the most natural light from the Sun, which is why it's easiest to see during the day, but light can also come from other sources like lamps or candles.

For example, look at the room below. Is it easy to see?

If the answer is yes, cup your hands around your eyes to block out the light and bring your face to the page.

Is it more difficult to see the details clearly?

Light enters your eye through your **pupil**. Your **iris**, the colored ring around your pupil, controls how *much* light enters your eye. If you look at your eyes in a mirror, you can see your pupils changing size. Your iris gets larger or smaller to adjust the amount of light entering your pupil.

PUPIL

IRIS

FACT! Brown eyes are the most common eye color in the world. Green eyes are the rarest.

7

Once light enters your eye through your pupil...

STEP 1
Your **cornea** and **lens** work together to focus the light. This is similar to how a magnifying glass works. Your cornea and lens aim the light at the back of your eye, which is called the **retina**.

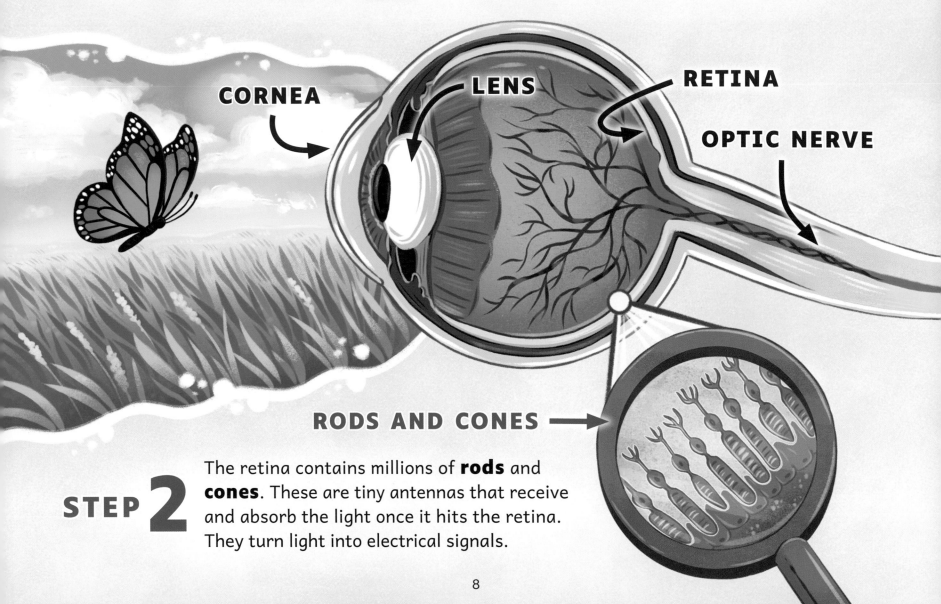

CORNEA

LENS

RETINA

OPTIC NERVE

RODS AND CONES

STEP 2
The retina contains millions of **rods** and **cones**. These are tiny antennas that receive and absorb the light once it hits the retina. They turn light into electrical signals.

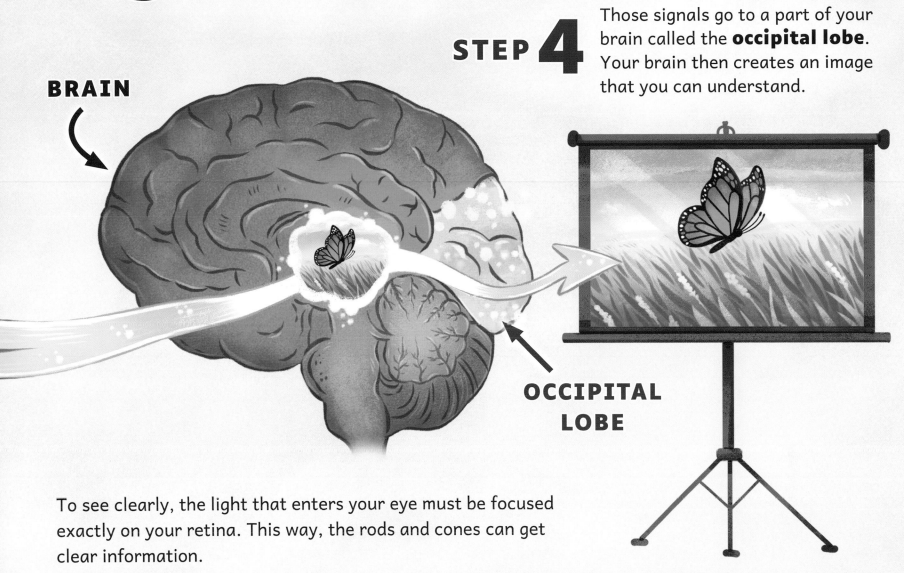

STEP 3 The electrical signals are sent to your brain through the **optic nerve.**

STEP 4 Those signals go to a part of your brain called the **occipital lobe**. Your brain then creates an image that you can understand.

BRAIN

OCCIPITAL LOBE

To see clearly, the light that enters your eye must be focused exactly on your retina. This way, the rods and cones can get clear information.

But what happens if light does not land on your retina?

The image you see becomes blurred.

When light is focused *in front* of the retina, this condition is called **myopia** or **nearsightedness**.

If you have myopia, you see the world clearly if it's close to you, but objects far away look blurry. It might be difficult for you to see the whiteboard in school. Luckily, myopia can be corrected with **prescription** lenses. These are glasses or **contact lenses** that you can get from an eye specialist, like an **optometrist**.

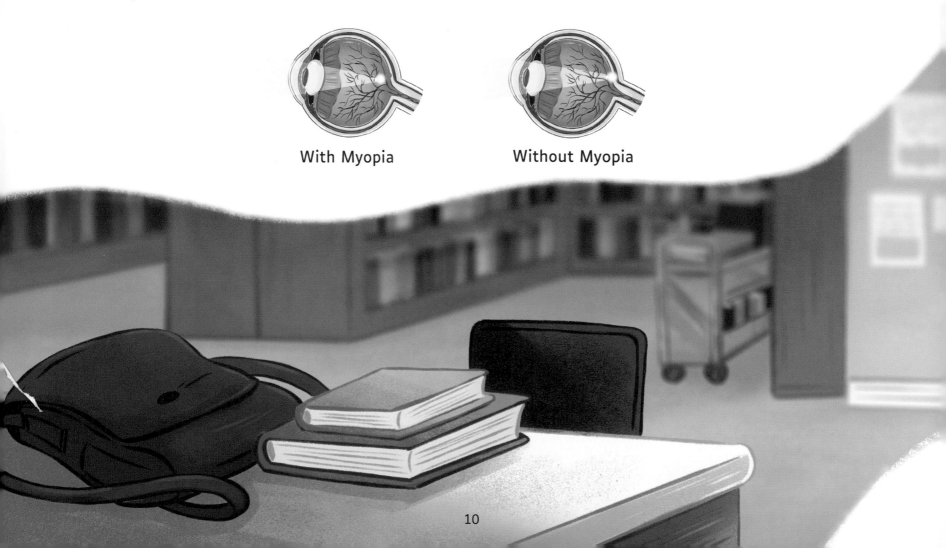

With Myopia   Without Myopia

Glasses and contact lenses refocus light so that it lands properly on your retina. To do that, they need to be made specifically for your eyes. If you have myopia, the lenses let you see objects in the distance more clearly. Can you see a difference if you look through the glasses in the picture?

 FACT! The most common vision test is called the **Snellen chart**. You read letters on the chart and are assigned a number, like 20/20 vision or 20/40 vision, based on how much of the chart you can read while standing 20 feet (6 meters) away.

In some cases, the eye focuses light *behind* the retina. This condition is known as **hyperopia**, which some people call **farsightedness**.

If you have hyperopia, you most likely see the world blurry up close while it is easier to see objects in the distance. You might have a hard time reading a quiz right in front of you, but be able to read the whiteboard or a poster far away.

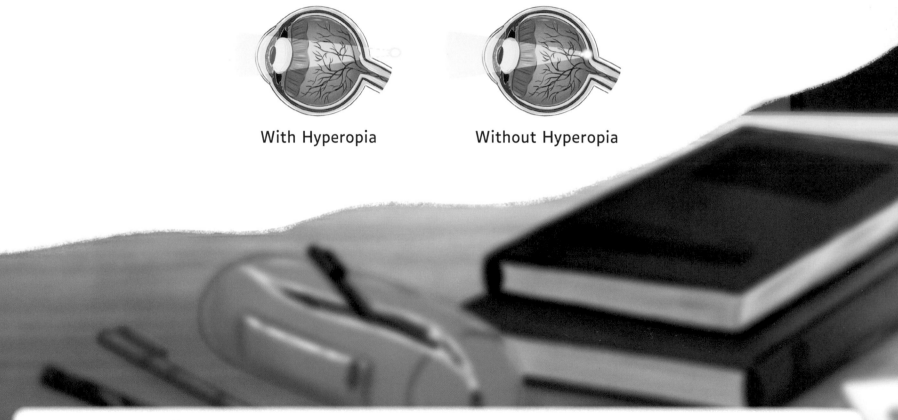

With Hyperopia   Without Hyperopia

 FACT! A similar condition to hyperopia is presbyopia. This condition can develop as we age, and it's more likely to affect people who already have hyperopia. If you notice an older relative holding a restaurant menu far away to read it, they might have presbyopia!

Just like for myopia, hyperopia can be corrected using prescription glasses or contacts. Wearing these specially designed lenses will make objects look clear, even when they are very close.

Light can also be focused on more than one spot at the same time, which happens when your cornea or lens is not shaped the way it should be. The light may land in front, behind, or on either side of the retina. This condition is called **astigmatism**.

If you have astigmatism, you see the world blurry or distorted at all distances. For example, a circle might look like an oval, and lights may have a fuzzy halo or glare.

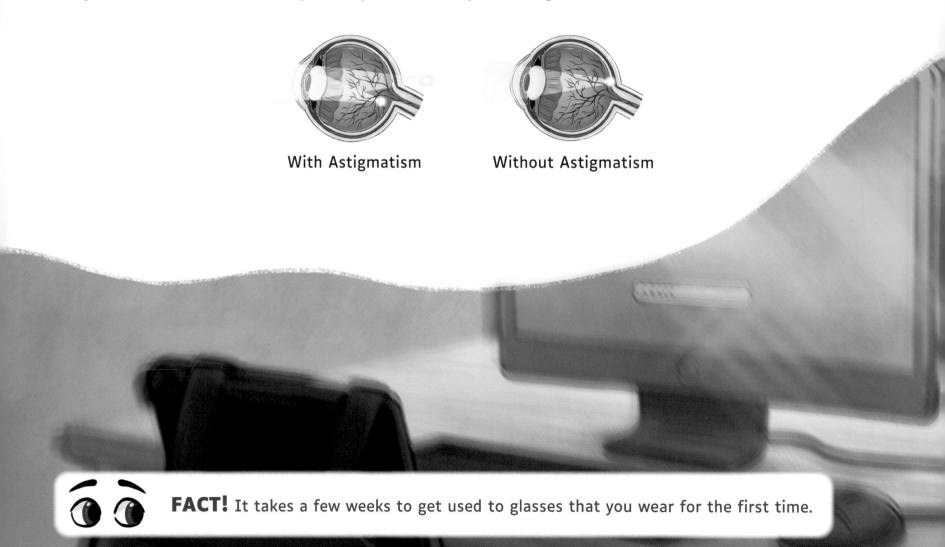

With Astigmatism   Without Astigmatism

FACT! It takes a few weeks to get used to glasses that you wear for the first time.

Lenses for astigmatism correct the focus of the light by making up for the shape of your cornea. For glasses, this means the thickness of the lens is uneven. For contacts, the shape of the lens is not a perfect circle. This is why contact lenses for astigmatism have tiny weights in them to make them stay in the right place on your eye.

Sometimes one eye focuses light differently than the other, or points in a slightly different direction. In each case, you end up with one "strong" eye that can see clearly and one "lazy" eye that doesn't focus as well. You then rely on the strong eye to see. This condition is called **amblyopia** or **lazy eye**.

If you have amblyopia, you see the world more clearly through one eye than through the other. You might have a hard time figuring out how far away things are, like when you're putting beads on a string or hitting a baseball.

Weak Eye   Strong Eye

There are a few ways to help correct amblyopia. Glasses or contact lenses can help the lazy eye focus. An eye doctor may also suggest doing eye exercises or wearing a patch over the strong eye to help strengthen the weaker eye.

FACT! When your eyes are misaligned, or pointing in slightly different directions, it's called strabismus. This is one of the main causes of amblyopia.

Even if your eyes focus light correctly, some of the light can be blocked before it reaches your retina, or parts of your eyes can be damaged. In these cases, it's possible to lose—or be born without—some or all of your vision.

If you are unable to see anything at all, it's called **total blindness**. However, most people who are considered blind can still see small amounts of light, shapes, and colors. If you have **low vision**, you can see more than someone who is blind, but you might have tunnel vision, blind spots, or blurriness that affect your daily life. Blindness and low vision can't be corrected with glasses or contacts.

Take a look at the image on this page.

Try holding your hands in a fist, leaving only a small gap like binoculars. Bring your hands up to your eyes.

Can you still see the picture? How much can you see?

Do you think it's difficult to do your homework or play outside if this is your everyday vision?

That's why there are tools and helpers that can assist you if you are blind or have low vision. Like:

CANES

A cane can help you walk confidently and avoid any obstacles. It also helps strangers understand that you need space. Canes are usually plain white or have red stripes, but they can be any color.

ASSISTIVE TECHNOLOGY

Technology like text-to-speech readers and portable braille readers help you read books or search online.

GUIDE DOGS

Guide dogs can alert you to potential danger, help you stay on a sidewalk or path, help you safely cross the street, and keep you from bumping into things.

PEOPLE

Family, friends, or trusted volunteers can walk with you and let you know what's ahead. They can also help with complicated activities like skiing!

A common thing that can reduce the amount of light that enters your eye is a **cataract**. This is when the clear lens in your eye becomes cloudy. Cataracts usually affect older people, but kids or babies can sometimes have them too. If they aren't treated, they can lead to complete vision loss.

If you have cataracts, you see the world as if you're looking through a foggy window, and it will get worse over time. If a person's pupils look gray or milky white, they likely have cataracts.

With Cataract   Without Cataract

Luckily, cataracts can be treated. Special eye doctors called **ophthalmologists** can remove the cloudy lens and replace it with an artificial lens. This eye surgery can restore your clear vision and keep you from going blind. Look through the eyes below to see what your vision would be like after surgery.

 FACT! You might have heard that carrots can improve your vision. It's true that carrots are good for keeping your eyes healthy, because they help you produce important vitamins, but they can't make you see better. This was a rumor spread during World War II.

Another condition that causes blindness is called **glaucoma**. With this condition, high pressure inside the eye damages the optic nerve that sends electrical signals to the brain. The eye might work fine in this case, but the brain doesn't get the full picture.

If you have glaucoma, you see the world as dim or blurry around the edges of your vision. You might notice this in an older relative who can't see things from the sides of their eyes.

With Glaucoma   Without Glaucoma

 FACT! Braille, named after its creator, Louis Braille, is a reading and writing system for people who are blind or have difficulty seeing. Braille is based on six raised dots used to make different characters that can be recognized by touch.

If it's caught early, glaucoma can be treated with special medication to control eye pressure. If it isn't caught in time, glaucoma will lead to permanent tunnel vision or total blindness.

If you go blind from glaucoma, you can't get your vision back. However, there are many tools and helpers available to you. Can you spot one or more helpers in the picture?

Can you see all of the words below?

In addition to issues with focus or the optic nerve, there can also be problems with the rods and cones in your retina. Remember, your rods and cones turn light into electrical signals for your brain.

 FACT! Your eyes are a type of organ called a "sense organ," which collects information about the world. The five sense organs are your eyes, ears, tongue, nose, and skin.

RODS

Rods are used in low light. They don't tell your brain anything about color, but they help you see shapes and shadows. A human eye has over *100 million* rods!

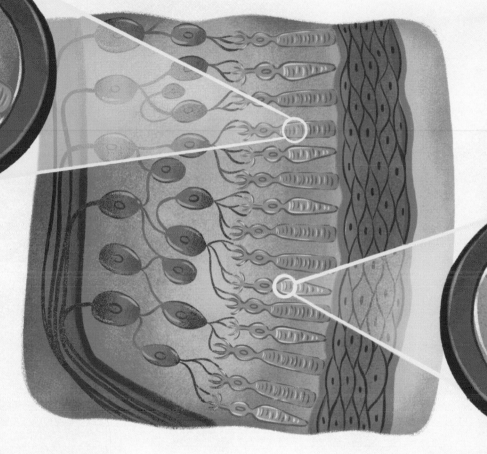

CONES

Cones, on the other hand, need good lighting to work, and they tell your brain about both the shapes and the colors you're seeing. There are a lot fewer cones than rods—each eye has around 6 million cones.

Cones need light to work, and light can be different colors.

White light, like sunlight, is actually a combination of all the visible colors. When white light hits an object, like a chair, only some of the colors **reflect**, or bounce off, the object. The color of the light that bounces off the object is the color that you see!

If the chair is red, that means red light is bouncing off it. When that red light reaches your eye and lands on your retina, your cones have the important job of telling your brain what color the chair is.

 FACT! At birth, babies are thought to see in black and white and shades of gray. Within a few months, as their brains develop, they get the ability to see color.

We have three different types of cones that pick up light. They are called **red**, **green**, or **blue** cones. Each type is sensitive to a different group of colors. Our brain combines information from all three types of cones to make even more colors—like mixing three shades of paint to get a new color. Altogether, we can see around a million different colors!

But does everyone see the world in the same colors?

Some people are born with missing or flawed cones. This is called **color vision deficiency** or **color blindness**. With fewer working cones, your brain has trouble telling certain colors apart.

If you have color blindness, the colors you see depend on whether it's your **red**, **green**, or **blue** cones that are not working. In rare cases, you might not see colors at all! Eye doctors can detect some types of color blindness with the **Ishihara test**. In this test, you look at pictures made up of colored dots, usually showing a number on a background. If you are missing red cones, it will be hard to see a red number on a green background.

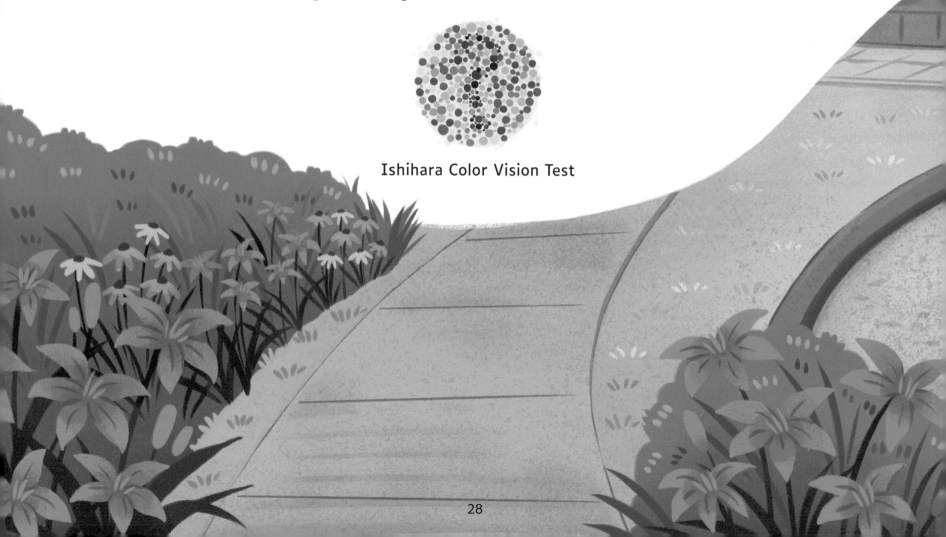

Ishihara Color Vision Test

While there is no cure for color blindness yet, there are glasses that can help. A filter in the lens blocks certain colors of light. This makes it easier for your brain to understand what colors you are seeing. Can you see any red in the playground below? How about when you look through the glasses?

 FACT! Color vision deficiency is sometimes called "Daltonism" after John Dalton, an English chemist, physicist, and meteorologist from the 18th century. Dalton was the first scientist to study color blindness after realizing that he saw color differently from others.

Even without a color vision deficiency, some colors can't be seen by the human eye. Colors like red, green, and blue are examples of **visible light**, but there are also types of **invisible light**.

Infrared light is one of those types. You can't see it, but you can feel it in the form of heat!

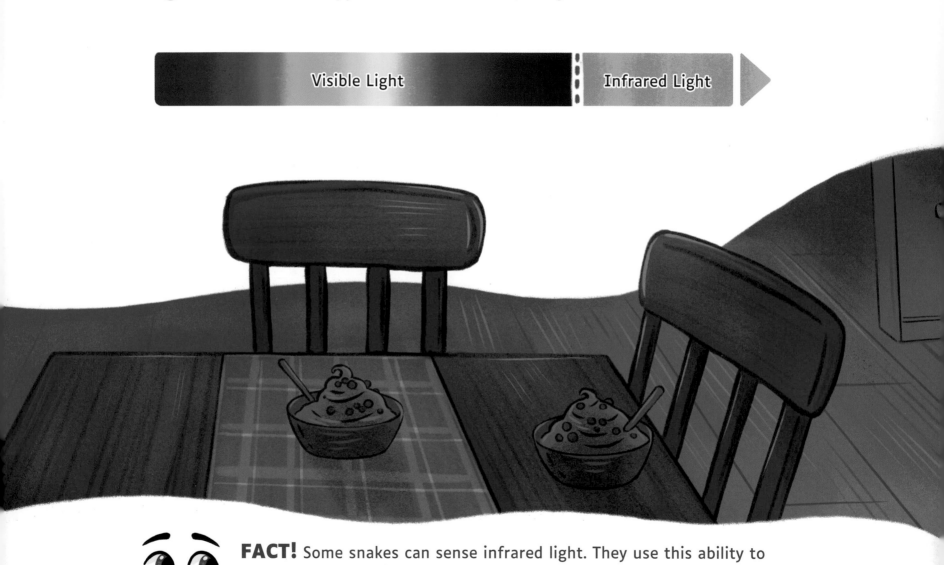

Visible Light

Infrared Light

FACT! Some snakes can sense infrared light. They use this ability to detect and hunt animals up to three feet (one meter) away from them.

All objects give off infrared light—warm things like a mug of cocoa give off more, and cold things like a glass of ice water give off less. Scientists have built cameras that can sense this invisible light and put together a picture for us, even in the dark. These devices are called thermal imaging cameras.

Infrared light is used in toasters and saunas to heat things up, and in other technology like television remote controls.

31

Ultraviolet light, or UV light, is another type of invisible light. The sun gives off ultraviolet light, but you can't see or feel it. However, UV light lets us see **fluorescent** objects, because it causes them to glow. There are some minerals, plants, and even animals that can be fluorescent.

UV Light | Visible Light

When you see glowing decorations in a bowling alley or theme park ride, the glow-in-the-dark effect is caused by UV light. It can make your white clothes or shoes glow too! UV light can be given off by special lightbulbs called blacklights.

 FACT! Bees can see ultraviolet light. They use this ability to find nectar and pollen at the center of flowers. Some fish can also see ultraviolet light and use it to detect zooplankton.

Over time, high exposure to ultraviolet light or infrared light can damage your eyes. Even bright sunlight can be bad for your vision. Similar to other parts of your body, eyes need to be protected.

Keep your eyes healthy:

- Make regular visits to the eye doctor. You might see an **optometrist** for a regular check-up or to get a prescription for glasses. You would visit an **optician** if you need to pick up new glasses, or an **ophthalmologist** if you have a serious eye condition.

- Eat fruits and vegetables to help protect your eyes and prevent vision loss. Carrots, apricots, sweet potatoes, spinach, and other foods rich in **beta-carotene** help with overall eye health.

- Reduce the brightness of light that comes from lamps or screens whenever you can.

- Take breaks from staring at a computer, phone, or tablet. You should take a break every 20 minutes to look at something 20 feet away (or 6 meters away) for 20 seconds. This is the 20-20-20 rule.

- When it's bright out, wear comfortable sunglasses made with UV protection. This reduces the damage to your eyes.

- Wear eye protection when there is any danger of something hitting or splashing in your eyes. Scientists wear goggles when they're working with chemicals, construction workers and engineers wear safety glasses to keep sharp materials from flying into their eyes, and athletes in sports like hockey wear helmets or goggles.

 FACT! Dolphins sleep with one eye open. When the right part of their brain rests, the left eye is closed, and vice versa.

You can see that our eyes are complex and fascinating.

It's important to know how they work so we can take good care of them and understand why each of us sees the world a little differently.

So... **how do YOU see the world?**

Glossary

Beta-carotene: a nutrient that helps your body produce vitamin A, which is important for eye health. It is found in carrots, spinach, sweet potatoes, broccoli, and other fruits and vegetables.

Cones: extremely small cells in the retina that turn light into electrical signals for your brain. Human eyes have three types of cones that work together to give your brain information about colors and shapes.

Contact lens: a round, curved piece of clear plastic that sits directly on your cornea. It focuses light to hit the retina so that you can see clearly.

Cornea: the clear outer layer of the eye that covers your iris and pupil. It helps focus light onto the retina.

Fluorescent: describes anything that gives off visible light after being exposed to ultraviolet light.

Invisible light: colors of light that cannot be seen by the human eye, but can be seen by some animals or sensed by special technology.

Iris: the colored ring around your pupil that controls how much light enters your eye.

Ishihara test: a way for eye doctors to tell if you have a red-green color vision deficiency. It is a series of numbers or patterns on circular backgrounds, which are made up of small dots in different colors.

Lens: the clear, inner part of your eye that sits behind your iris and pupil and focuses light onto the retina. Also, any clear object that focuses light (like a contact lens or the lens of your glasses).

Occipital lobe: the part of your brain that reads information sent from your eyes and instantly puts together an image you can understand.

Ophthalmologist: an eye doctor who can prescribe lenses and medications, recommend eye exercises, and perform eye surgery.

Optic nerve: a part of the nervous system that carries electrical signals from your eyes to your brain.

Optometrist: an eye specialist who can test for eye conditions, recommend eye exercises, treat minor injuries, and prescribe lenses.

Optician: a professional who can fit you for glasses or contact lenses, making sure you get the prescription recommended by your eye doctor.

Prescription: a treatment, like glasses or medicine, that you can only get with permission from a doctor.

Pupil: the black hole in the center of your iris that allows light to enter your eye.

Reflect: to bounce off something and change directions, such as light bouncing off a mirror.

Retina: the inner surface of the back of your eye, which holds millions of rods and cones.

Rods: extremely small cells in the retina that turn light into electrical signals for your brain. They give your brain information about shapes, but not about color.

Snellen chart: a way for eye doctors to tell if you are nearsighted, or to tell how nearsighted you are. It is a poster with rows of letters that are larger at the top than at the bottom.

Visible light: colors of light that can be seen by the human eye.

White light: light that appears colorless, like sunlight, but actually contains all the colors of the rainbow.

About the Author and Illustrator

"To my grandmother, who made me appreciate how much she could see and give despite being blind."

Noureddine Melikechi is an optical physicist, educator, and inventor. A physics professor at the University of Massachusetts, Lowell, he also serves as Dean of the Kennedy College of Sciences. He works on the interaction of light with various types of matter. Noureddine has researched using light to detect early signs of disease including cancers. A native of Algeria, Noureddine received his *Diplôme d'Études Supérieures* in Physics from the *Université des sciences et de la technologie Houari-Boumediene*, Algeria, and his M.Sc. and D.Phil., both in Physics, from the University of Sussex, England. He can be reached at Noureddine.Melikechi@ScienceNaturally.com.

"To my dad, who has struggled with double vision since his cancer, and to all of the kids in the ophthalmology waiting room he sat with over the years; I hope this book helps you understand and love your eyes!"

Michelle Simpson is a full-time freelance illustrator, focusing mainly on children's books. Some notable publications include *I Can See You* by Rosemarie Avrana Meyok, the *Jordan and Max* series By Suzanne Sutherland, and *Talloqut: A Story from West Greenland* by Paninnguaq Lind Jensen. She has also worked as a concept artist for kids' cartoons such as *Ollie! The Boy Who Became What He Ate* (season two), *Tee and Mo* (season one) and *Happy House of Frightenstein* (season one). Michelle holds a BAA in illustration from Sheridan College in Ontario, and she lives on the Canadian side of Niagara Falls. You can see more of her work at MichelleScribbles.com